BORROWER'S NAME	ROOM NO.
DATE DUE		16
101	Damaris	

WEEKLY **WR** READER®
EARLY LEARNING LIBRARY

Animals That Live in the Mountains/
Animales de las montañas

Bighorn Sheep/
Carnero de Canadá

by/por JoAnn Early Macken

Reading consultant/Consultora de lectura:
Susan Nations, M.Ed.,
author/literacy coach/consultant in literacy development
autora/tutora de alfabetización/
consultora de desarrollo de la lectura

Please visit our web site at: www.earlyliteracy.cc
For a free color catalog describing Weekly Reader® Early Learning Library's list
of high-quality books, call 1-877-445-5824 (USA) or 1-800-387-3178 (Canada).
Weekly Reader® Early Learning Library's fax: (414) 336-0164.

Library of Congress Cataloging-in-Publication Data

Macken, JoAnn Early, 1953-
    [Bighorn sheep. Spanish & English]
    Bighorn sheep = Carnero de Canadá / by JoAnn Early Macken.
        p. cm. — (Animals that live in the mountains = Animales de las montañas)
    Includes bibliographical references and index.
    ISBN 0-8368-6446-8 (lib. bdg.)
    ISBN 0-8368-6453-0 (softcover)
    1. Bighorn sheep—Juvenile literature. I. Title: Carnero de Canadá. II. Title.
    QL737.U53M215   2006
    599.649'7—dc22   2005033300

This edition first published in 2006 by
Weekly Reader® Early Learning Library
A Member of the WRC Media Family of Companies
330 West Olive Street, Suite 100
Milwaukee, WI 53212 USA

Copyright © 2006 by Weekly Reader® Early Learning Library

Managing editor: Valerie J. Weber
Art direction: Tammy West
Cover design and page layout: Kami Strunsee
Picture research: Diane Laska-Swanke
Translators: Tatiana Acosta and Guillermo Gutiérrez

Picture credits: Cover, pp. 7, 15, 19, 21 © Tom and Pat Leeson; p. 5 © Alan & Sandy Carey;
pp. 9, 11, 13, 17 © Michael H. Francis

Printed in the United States of America

1 2 3 4 5 6 7 8 9 10 09 08 07 06

Note to Educators and Parents

Reading is such an exciting adventure for young children! They are beginning to integrate their oral language skills with written language. To encourage children along the path to early literacy, books must be colorful, engaging, and interesting; they should invite the young reader to explore both the print and the pictures.

Animals That Live in the Mountains is a new series designed to help children read about creatures that make their homes in high places. Each book describes a different mountain animal's life cycle, behavior, and habitat.

Each book is specially designed to support the young reader in the reading process. The familiar topics are appealing to young children and invite them to read — and reread — again and again. The full-color photographs and enhanced text further support the student during the reading process.

In addition to serving as wonderful picture books in schools, libraries, homes, and other places where children learn to love reading, these books are specifically intended to be read within an instructional guided reading group. This small group setting allows beginning readers to work with a fluent adult model as they make meaning from the text. After children develop fluency with the text and content, the book can be read independently. Children and adults alike will find these books supportive, engaging, and fun!

— Susan Nations, M.Ed., author, literacy coach,
and consultant in literacy development

Nota para los maestros y los padres

¡Leer es una aventura tan emocionante para los niños pequeños! A esta edad están comenzando a integrar su manejo del lenguaje oral con el lenguaje escrito. Para animar a los niños en el camino de la lectura incipiente, los libros deben ser coloridos, estimulantes e interesantes; deben invitar a los jóvenes lectores a explorar la letra impresa y las ilustraciones.

Animales de las montañas es una nueva colección diseñada para presentar a los jóvenes lectores algunos animales que viven en regiones montañosas. Cada libro explica, en un lenguaje sencillo y fácil de leer, el ciclo de vida, el comportamiento y el hábitat de un animal de las montañas.

Cada libro está especialmente diseñado para ayudar a los jóvenes lectores en el proceso de lectura. Los temas familiares llaman la atención de los niños y los invitan a leer — y releer — una y otra vez. Las fotografías a todo color y el tamaño de la letra ayudan aún más al estudiante en el proceso de lectura.

Además de servir como maravillosos libros ilustrados en escuelas, bibliotecas, hogares y otros lugares donde los niños aprenden a amar la lectura, estos libros han sido especialmente concebidos para ser leídos en un grupo de lectura guiada. Este contexto permite que los lectores incipientes trabajen con un adulto que domina la lectura mientras van determinando el significado del texto. Una vez que los niños dominan el texto y el contenido, el libro puede ser leído de manera independiente. ¡Estos libros les resultarán útiles, estimulantes y divertidos a niños y a adultos por igual!

— Susan Nations, M.Ed., autora/tutora de alfabetización/
consultora de desarrollo de la lectura

A bighorn sheep can stand soon after it is born. A baby, or **lamb**, can walk in a few hours. Soon it can run and jump. A female sheep, or **ewe**, feeds her lamb milk.

━━━━━━━━━━━━━━━━━━━━

Un carnero de Canadá puede ponerse en pie poco después de nacer. La cría, o **cordero**, puede caminar en unas horas. Poco después puede correr y saltar. El carnero hembra alimenta con leche a su cordero.

In a few months, lambs eat grass.
Sheep swallow their food in quick bites.
Later, they bring it up to chew it. Then
they swallow it again.

En pocos meses, los corderos comen
pasto. Los carneros se tragan la
comida deprisa. Más tarde, la
recuperan para masticarla, y se la
vuelven a tragar.

Ewes and lambs stay in a group.
Lambs play with each other. Males,
or **rams**, also stay in a group. One
sheep watches out for danger.

━ ━ ━ ━ ━ ━ ━ ━ ━ ━ ━ ━ ━ ━ ━ ━ ━

Las hembras y los corderos van en
grupo. Los corderos juguetean juntos.
Los machos también van en grupo.
Uno de ellos vigila por si hay peligro.

9

Bighorns can see far away. If a ewe sees danger, she stamps her foot. If a ram sees danger, he snorts. The group runs down the mountain.

Los carneros pueden ver a gran distancia. Si una hembra ve un peligro, patea el suelo. Si un macho ve un peligro, resopla. El grupo escapa corriendo montaña abajo.

11

Bighorns are good at climbing. Their feet do not slip. Sheep leap from rock to rock. They jump off high cliffs!

Los carneros trepan bien. Sus patas no se resbalan. Brincan de roca en roca. ¡Saltan de altos precipicios!

13

A bighorn sheep's horns keep growing.
A ram's horns grow back and down.
They can curl into circles.

Los cuernos de un carnero de
Canadá no dejan de crecer. Los
cuernos del macho crecen hacia
atrás y hacia abajo. Pueden llegar
a formar círculos.

ram/
macho

ewe/
hembra

15

Rams fight with their horns. Crash!
They slam into each other!

Los machos luchan con los cuernos.
¡Bum! ¡Chocan uno contra el otro!

17

In winter, snow can cover the grass. Sheep scrape away the snow. A group may move to a place with less snow.

En el invierno, la nieve puede cubrir el pasto. Los carneros apartan la nieve rascando con las patas. Un grupo puede irse a otro lugar con menos nieve.

19

Bighorns grow heavy coats for winter.
In spring, they **shed**, or lose, some hair.
They look for green grass to eat.

━ ━ ━ ━ ━ ━ ━ ━ ━ ━ ━ ━ ━ ━ ━ ━ ━ ━

A los carneros les crece una capa
densa de pelo en el invierno. En la
primavera, la **mudan**, y pierden algo
de pelo. Entonces buscan pasto verde
para comer.

Glossary

cliffs — steep rock faces

danger — a thing that may cause harm or pain

scrape — to scratch or rub with something sharp

snorts — makes a sound by blowing air out through the nose

swallow — to pass through the mouth to the stomach while eating

Glosario

precipicios — altas paredes de roca

peligro — algo que puede causar daño o dolor

rascar — restregar con algo afilado

resoplar — hacer ruido echando aire por la nariz

tragar — hacer que algo pase desde la boca hasta el estómago mientras se come

For More Information/Más información

Books

Bighorn Sheep. Aaron Frisch (Smart Apple Media)

The Bighorn Sheep. Wildlife of North America (series). Joanne Mattern (Capstone)

Libros

Ovejas (Sheep). Animales de la granja/Farm Animals (series). Peter Brady (Bridgestone)

Sheep/Las ovejas. Animals That Live on the Farm/ Animales que viven en la granja (series). JoAnn Early Macken (Weekly Reader Early Learning Library)

Web Sites/Páginas web

Big Horn Sheep
Carneros de Canadá
www.nature.ca/notebooks/english/bighorn.htm
Illustration and facts about bighorn sheep
Ilustraciones y datos sobre el carnero de Canadá

23

Index

Índice

About the Author

JoAnn Early Macken is the author of two rhyming picture books, *Sing-Along Song* and *Cats on Judy*, and more than eighty nonfiction books for children. Her poems have appeared in several children's magazines. A graduate of the M.F.A. in Writing for Children and Young Adults Program at Vermont College, she lives in Wisconsin with her husband and their two sons.

Información sobre la autora

JoAnn Early Macken ha escrito dos libros de rimas con ilustraciones, *Sing-Along Song* y *Cats on Judy*, y más de ochenta libros de no ficción para niños. Sus poemas han sido publicados en varias revistas infantiles. JoAnn se graduó en el programa M.F.A de Escritura para Niños y Jóvenes de Vermont College. Vive en Wisconsin con su esposo y sus dos hijos.